...excellent ... with love
and my wishes for a
wonderful life.
love
Pam

Come, Listen to
a Prophet's Voice

Come, Listen to a Prophet's Voice

Ezra Taft Benson

Deseret Book Company
Salt Lake City, Utah

©1990 Deseret Book Company

All rights reserved. No part of this book may be reproduced in any form or by any means without permission in writing from the publisher, Deseret Book Company, P.O. Box 30178, Salt Lake City, Utah 84130.

Deseret Book is a registered trademark of Deseret Book Company.

Library of Congress Catalog Card No. 89-82729

ISBN 0-87579-351-7

Printed in the United States of America

10   9   8   7   6   5   4   3   2   1

Contents

Publisher's Foreword

On 5 April 1986, President Ezra Taft Benson addressed the young men of The Church of Jesus Christ of Latter-day Saints. That was the beginning of a series of eight talks delivered to those in the Church of various ages and interests, the last being given on 30 September 1989 to the elderly. Few talks have had as much influence on Church members today as those eight talks. In a world of shifting values and roles, President Benson clearly defined the responsibilities and challenges of children, youth, single adults, parents, and the elderly and lovingly proffered the Lord's direction and encouragement.

All eight addresses are included in this volume in the order they were given. Because of the breadth and scope of the prophet's messages in this series, every member of the Church of any age or circumstance will be touched and blessed by his inspired counsel.

To the Young Men of the Priesthood

An address given at the priesthood session of general conference, 5 April 1986

My beloved brethren, this has been a glorious meeting.

I have been especially pleased to see the number of young men in attendance this evening. With all my heart I love the youth of the Church. I have spent much of my life in their service, and their well-being and happiness are among my greatest concerns.

Tonight I would like to speak directly to you young men of the Aaronic Priesthood. I am grateful that many of your fathers and priesthood leaders are with you, for I would like them to hear my message also.

Young men of the Aaronic Priesthood, you have been born at this time for a sacred and glorious purpose. It is not by chance that you have been reserved to come to earth in this last dispensation of the fulness of times. Your birth at this particular time was foreordained in the eternities.

You are to be the royal army of the Lord in the last days. You are "youth of the noble birthright." ("Carry On," in *Hymns of The Church of Jesus Christ of Latter-day Saints* [Salt Lake City: The Church of Jesus Christ of Latter-day Saints, 1985], no. 255.)

In the spiritual battles you are waging, I see you as today's sons of Helaman. Remember well the Book of Mormon account of Helaman's two thousand stripling warriors and how the teachings of their mothers

1

gave them strength and faith. These marvelous mothers taught them to put on the whole armor of God, to place their trust in the Lord, and to doubt not. By so doing, not one of these young men was lost. (See Alma 53:10–23; 56:41–56.)

My young brethren, I counsel each of you to draw close to your own mother. Respect her. Honor her. Receive your mother's counsel as she loves and instructs you in righteousness. And honor and obey your father as he stands as the head of the home, emulating his manly qualities.

Young men, the family unit is forever, and you should do everything in your power to strengthen that unit. In your own family, encourage family home evenings and be an active participant. Encourage family prayer and be on your knees with your family in that sacred circle. Do your part to develop real family unity and solidarity. In such homes, there is no generation gap.

Your most important friendships should be with your own brothers and sisters and with your father and mother. Love your family. Be loyal to them. Have a genuine concern for your brothers and sisters. Help carry their load so you can say, like the lyrics of that song, "He ain't heavy; he's my brother." (Bob Russell, "He Ain't Heavy" [Lynbrook, New York: Harrison Music Corporation, 1969].)

Remember, the family is one of God's greatest fortresses against the evils of our day. Help keep your family strong and close and worthy of our Father in Heaven's blessings. As you do, you will receive faith and strength, which will bless your lives forever.

Next, young men, may I admonish you to participate in a program of daily reading and pondering of the scriptures. We remember the experience of our beloved prophet, President Spencer W. Kimball. As a fourteen-year-old boy, he accepted the challenge of reading the Bible from cover to cover. Most of his reading was done by coal oil light in his attic bedroom. He read every night until he completed the 1,519 pages, which took him approximately a year; but he attained his goal.

Of the four great standard works of the Church — the Bible, the Book of Mormon, the Doctrine and Covenants, and the Pearl of Great Price — I would particularly urge you to read again and again the Book of Mormon and ponder and apply its teachings. The Book of Mormon was referred to by the Prophet Joseph Smith as "the most correct of any book on earth, and the keystone of our religion." (*History of The Church of Jesus Christ of Latter-day Saints,* 2nd ed. rev., 7 vols. [Salt Lake City: The Church of Jesus Christ of Latter-day Saints, 1932–51], 4:461.)

Young men, the Book of Mormon will change your life. It will fortify you against the evils of our day. It will bring a spirituality into your life that no other book will. It will be the most important book you will read in preparation for a mission and for life. A young man who knows and loves the Book of Mormon, who has read it several times, who has an abiding testimony of its truthfulness, and who applies its teachings will be able to stand against the wiles of the devil and will be a mighty tool in the hands of the Lord.

Further, I would encourage you brethren of the Aaronic Priesthood to receive a patriarchal blessing. Study it carefully and regard it as personal scripture to you — for that is what it is. A patriarchal blessing is the inspired and prophetic statement of your life's mission together with blessings, cautions, and admonitions as the patriarch may be prompted to give.

3

(See James R. Clark, comp., *Messages of the First Presidency of The Church of Jesus Christ of Latter-day Saints,* 6 vols. [Salt Lake City: Bookcraft, 1965–75], 6:194.) Young men, receive your patriarchal blessing under the influence of fasting and prayer, and then read it regularly that you may know God's will for you.

May I now direct your attention to the importance of attending all of your Church meetings. Faithful attendance at Church meetings brings blessings you can receive in no other way.

Attend your sacrament meeting every Sunday. Listen carefully to the messages. Pray for the spirit of understanding and testimony. Be worthy to prepare and bless and pass the sacrament. Come to the sacrament table with clean hands and a pure heart.

Attend your Sunday School classes every Sunday. Listen carefully to the lesson and participate in class discussions. Gospel scholarship and an increase in testimony will result.

Attend your priesthood quorum meetings every Sunday, and your quorum activities held on weeknights. Learn well your priesthood responsibilities, and then perform them with diligence and reverence.

Young men, take full advantage of the Church programs. Set your goals to attain excellence in the achievement programs of the Church. Earn the Duty to God Award — one of our most significant priesthood awards. Become an Eagle Scout. Do not settle for mediocrity in the great Scouting program of the Church.

Regularly attend seminary and be a seminary graduate. Seminary instruction is one of the most significant spiritual experiences a young man can have.

May I now speak with you about missionary service in the kingdom. I feel very deeply about this. I pray that you will understand the yearnings of my heart. The Prophet Joseph Smith declared, "After all that has been said, [our] greatest and most important duty is to preach the Gospel." (*Teachings of the Prophet Joseph Smith,* sel. by Joseph Fielding Smith [Salt Lake City: Deseret Book Company, 1938], 113.)

The Lord wants every young man to serve a full-time mission. Currently, only a fifth of the eligible young men in the Church are serving full-time missions. This is not pleasing to the Lord. We can do better. We *must* do better.

Not only should a mission be regarded as a priesthood duty, but every young man should look forward to this experience with great joy and anticipation. What a privilege—what a sacred privilege—to serve the Lord full time for two years with all your heart, might, mind, and strength.

You can do nothing more important. School can wait. Scholarships can be deferred. Occupational goals can be postponed. Yes, even temple marriage should wait until after a young man has served an honorable full-time mission for the Lord. And I would admonish you to date only faithful young women who also believe this and give you that encouragement.

Young men, look forward to full-time missionary service. Show your love and commitment to the Lord by responding to His call to serve. Know that the real purpose in going into the mission field is to bring souls unto Christ, to teach and baptize our Heavenly Father's children so that you may rejoice with them in the kingdom of our Father. (See D&C 18:15.) Prepare now for your mission by doing these things we have discussed this evening.

Another vital ingredient in preparation for your mission is to always live a clean life. We want morally clean young men in the mission field. We want you to live the clean life all of your life. We want the morally clean life to be your way of life.

Yes, one can repent of moral transgression. The miracle of forgiveness is real, and true repentance is accepted of the Lord. But it is not pleasing to the Lord prior to a mission, or at any time, to sow one's wild oats, to engage in sexual transgression of any nature, and then to expect that planned confession and quick repentance will satisfy the Lord.

President Kimball was emphatic on this point. In his marvelous book *The Miracle of Forgiveness,* he stated: "That man who resists temptation and lives without sin is far better off than the man who has fallen, no matter how repentant the latter may be. . . . How much better it is never to have committed sin!" (Salt Lake City: Bookcraft, 1969, 357.)

One of our fine stake presidents shared with us the following experience:

"I remember a girl that I had gone to high school with. She was from a good LDS family, but when she was a junior in high school, she began to compromise her standards and principles.

"I remember how stunned I was one afternoon as a group of us were in the back of the bus, riding home from school, and we were talking about the consequences of sin or transgression. And she flatly announced that she wasn't worried about committing any sin because her bishop had told her she could easily repent and could be quickly forgiven.

"Well, I was shocked with this flippant attitude that didn't reflect any understanding of repentance or appreciation of the miracle of forgiveness. I was also sure that she had grossly misunderstood the instruction and counsel of her bishop."

Adultery, or anything like unto it, is abominable

in the sight of the Lord. President Kimball also wisely observed:

"Among the most common sexual sins our young people commit are necking and petting. Not only do these improper relations often lead to fornication, pregnancy, and abortion—all ugly sins—but in and of themselves they are pernicious evils, and it is often difficult for youth to distinguish where one ends and another begins. . . .

"Too often, young people dismiss their petting with a shrug of their shoulders as a *little* indiscretion, while admitting that fornication is a base transgression. Too many of them are shocked, or feign to be, when told that what they have done in the name of petting was in reality [a form of] fornication." (*Miracle of Forgiveness,* 65–66.)

Young men of the Aaronic Priesthood, remember the scriptural injunction, "Be ye clean that bear the vessels of the Lord." (3 Ne. 20:41; D&C 38:42; see also Isa. 52:11.) Remember the story of Joseph in Egypt, who hearkened not to the wife of Potiphar and maintained his purity and virtue. (See Gen. 39:6–20).

Consider carefully the words of the prophet Alma to his errant son, Corianton, "Forsake your sins, and go no more after the lusts of your eyes." (Alma 39:9.)

"The lusts of your eyes." In our day, what does that expression mean?

Movies, television programs, and video recordings that are both suggestive and lewd.

Magazines and books that are obscene and pornographic.

We counsel you, young men, not to pollute your minds with such degrading matter, for the mind through which this filth passes is never the same afterward. Don't see R-rated movies or vulgar videos

7

or participate in any entertainment that is immoral, suggestive, or pornographic. Don't listen to music that is degrading. Remember Elder Boyd K. Packer's statement:

"Music, once . . . innocent, now is often used for wicked purposes. . . .

"In our day music itself has been corrupted. Music can, by its tempo, by its beat, by its intensity [and I would add, by its lyrics], dull the spiritual sensitivity of men. . . .

"Young people," Elder Packer goes on to say, "you cannot afford to fill your mind with the unworthy hard music of our day." ("Inspiring Music — Worthy Thoughts," *Ensign,* January 1974, 25, 28.)

Instead, we encourage you to listen to uplifting music, both popular and classical, that builds the spirit. Learn some favorite hymns from our new hymnbook that build faith and spirituality. Attend dances where the music and the lighting and the dance movements are conducive to the Spirit. Watch those shows and entertainment that lift the spirit and promote clean thoughts and actions. Read books and magazines that do the same.

And remember, young men, the importance of proper dating. President Kimball gave some wise counsel on this subject:

"Clearly, right marriage begins with right dating. . . . Therefore, this warning comes with great emphasis. Do not take the chance of dating nonmembers, or members who are untrained and faithless. [You] may say, 'Oh, I do not intend to marry this person. It is just a "fun" date.' But one cannot afford to take a chance on falling in love with someone who may never accept the gospel." (*Miracle of Forgiveness,* 241–42.)

8

Our Heavenly Father wants you to date young women who are faithful members of the Church, who encourage you to serve a full-time mission and to magnify your priesthood.

Yes, prepare well for a mission all your life, not just six months or a year before you go.

We love all of our missionaries who are serving the Lord full time in the mission field. But there is a difference in missionaries. Some are better prepared to serve the Lord the first month in the mission field than some who are returning home after twenty-four months.

We want young men entering the mission field who can enter the mission field "on the run," who have the faith born of personal righteousness and clean living that they can have a great and productive mission. We want missionaries who have the kind of faith that Wilford Woodruff and Heber C. Kimball had, each bringing hundreds and thousands of souls into the waters of baptism.

Give me a young man who has kept himself morally clean and has faithfully attended his Church meetings. Give me a young man who has magnified his priesthood and has earned the Duty to God Award and is an Eagle Scout. Give me a young man who is a seminary graduate and has a burning testimony of the Book of Mormon. Give me such a young man, and I will give you a young man who can perform miracles for the Lord in the mission field and throughout his life.

Now I would like to say a final word to the fathers and priesthood leaders in attendance this evening. Fathers, stay close to your sons. Earn and deserve their love and respect. Be united with their mother in the rearing of your children. Do nothing in your life

9

to cause your sons to stumble because of your example. Guide your sons. Teach them.

As I indicated last October as we met in general priesthood session, you have the major responsibility for teaching your sons the gospel. I would encourage you to reread that address. As important as the organizations of the Church are for teaching our youth, fathers have a sacred calling to continually teach and instruct members of their families in the principles of the gospel of Jesus Christ.

Priesthood leaders, remember that the bishop is the president of the Aaronic Priesthood. Bishops, your first and foremost responsibility is the Aaronic Priesthood and the young women of your wards.

Stay close to your young men. Get inside their lives. A personal interview once a year with them is not sufficient to fulfill your sacred duty. Visit with them often. Attend their quorum and Scout meetings. Go on their campouts. Participate in their youth conferences. Promote father-and-son activities. Talk with them often about a mission, and regularly visit with them about their personal worthiness.

Strengthen the Aaronic Priesthood quorums. Effectively use the videotape entitled "Vitalizing the Aaronic Priesthood Quorums" and the accompanying training guide. These are some of the finest training tools we have in the Aaronic Priesthood. Bishoprics, quorum advisers, and quorum presidencies should regularly use this training program.

Now, in closing, my young men of the Aaronic Priesthood, how I love you, how I respect you, how I pray for you. Remember the counsel I have given you tonight. It is what the Lord would have you hear now—today.

Live up to your godly potential. Remember who

you are and the priesthood that you bear. Be modern-day sons of Helaman. Put on the whole armor of God. "O youth of the noble birthright," with all my heart I say, "Carry on, carry on, carry on!" (*Hymns*, no. 255.) In the name of Jesus Christ, amen.

To the
Young Women
of the Church

An address given at the general women's
meeting of the Church, 27 September 1986

My dear sisters, this has been a glorious meeting. What an opportunity to meet with the choice daughters of our Father in Heaven gathered in meetinghouses throughout the world!

Last April general conference I had a similar opportunity to speak to all the men of the Church on Saturday evening in general priesthood meeting. At that time, I spoke directly to the Aaronic Priesthood. Tonight, I would like to speak to you young women of corresponding age.

Some of what I say this evening will be exactly what I said to the young men six months ago, and which I want you to know likewise applies directly to you. I shall discuss other matters with you this evening that apply only to you, as young sisters, and your sacred callings as daughters of our Father in Heaven.

President David O. McKay said, "There is nothing so sacred as true womanhood." (David O. McKay, *Gospel Ideals: Selections from the Discourses of David O. McKay* [Salt Lake City: Improvement Era, 1953], 353.) I agree with that statement with all my heart.

I appreciate so much the theme of your meeting this evening, "Abound in Hope." It is an inspired theme.

13

What hopes I have for you young sisters! What hopes our Father in Heaven has for you!

You have been born at this time for a sacred and glorious purpose. It is not by chance that you have been reserved to come to earth in this last dispensation of the fulness of times. Your birth at this particular time was foreordained in the eternities.

You are to be the royal daughters of the Lord in the last days. You are "youth of the noble birthright." ("Carry On," in *Hymns of The Church of Jesus Christ of Latter-day Saints* [Salt Lake City: The Church of Jesus Christ of Latter-day Saints, 1985], no. 255.)

My young sisters, I am happy to see so many of you with your mothers this evening. I counsel each of you to draw close to your own mother. Love her. Respect her. Honor her. Receive your mother's counsel as she loves and instructs you in righteousness. Honor and obey your father as he stands as the head of the home by emulating his spiritual qualities.

Young women, the family unit is forever, and you should do everything in your power to strengthen that unit. In your own family, encourage family home evenings and be an active participant. Encourage family prayer. Be on your knees with your family in that sacred circle. Do your part to develop real family unity and solidarity.

In such homes there is no generation gap. That is another tool of the devil. Your most important friendships should be with your own brothers and sisters and with your father and mother. Love your family. Be loyal to them. Have a genuine concern for your brothers and sisters. Help carry their load so you can say, as in the lyrics of that song, "He ain't heavy; he's my brother." (Bob Russell, "He Ain't Heavy" [Lynbrook, New York: Harrison Music Corporation, 1969].)

Remember, the family is one of God's greatest fortresses against the evils of our day.

Help keep your family strong and close and worthy of our Father in Heaven's blessings. As you do, you will receive faith and hope and strength, which will bless your lives forever.

Next, young women, may I admonish you to participate in a program of daily reading and pondering of the scriptures. We remember the experience of our beloved prophet, President Spencer W. Kimball. As a fourteen-year-old boy, he accepted the challenge of reading the Bible from cover to cover. Most of his reading was done by coal oil light in his attic bedroom. He read every night until he completed the 1,519 pages, which took him approximately a year; but he attained his goal.

Of the four great standard works of the Church—the Bible, the Book of Mormon, the Doctrine and Covenants, and the Pearl of Great Price—I would particularly urge you to read again and again the Book of Mormon and ponder and apply its teachings. The Book of Mormon was referred to by the Prophet Joseph Smith as "the most correct of any book on earth, and the keystone of our religion, and a man [and woman] would get nearer to God by abiding by its precepts, than by any other book." (*History of The Church of Jesus Christ of Latter-day Saints,* 2nd ed. rev., 7 vols. [Salt Lake City: The Church of Jesus Christ of Latter-day Saints, 1932–51], 4:461.)

Young women, the Book of Mormon will change your life. It will fortify you against the evils of our day. It will bring a spirituality into your life that no other book will. It will be the most important book you will read in preparation for life's challenges. A young woman who knows and loves the Book of Mormon, who has read it several times, who has an abiding testimony of its truthfulness, and who applies its teachings will be able to stand against the wiles of the devil and will be a mighty tool in the hands of the Lord.

Further, I would encourage you, young sisters, as you approach your teenage years, to receive a patriarchal blessing. Study it carefully and regard it as personal scripture to you—for that indeed is what it is. A patriarchal blessing is "an inspired and prophetic statement of [your life's] mission . . . together with such blessings, cautions, and admonitions as the patriarch may be prompted to give." (James R. Clark, comp., *Messages of the First Presidency of The Church of Jesus Christ of Latter-day Saints,* 6 vols. [Salt Lake City: Bookcraft, 1965–75], 6:194.)

Young women, receive your patriarchal blessings under the influence of fasting and prayer, and then read it regularly that you may know God's will for you.

May I now direct your attention to the importance of attending all of your Church meetings. Faithful attendance at Church meetings brings blessings you can receive in no other way.

Attend your sacrament meeting every Sunday. Listen carefully to the messages. Pray for the spirit of understanding and testimony. Partake of the sacrament with clean hands and a pure heart.

Attend your Sunday School classes every Sunday. Listen carefully to the lessons and participate in class discussions. Gospel scholarship and an increase in testimony will result.

Attend your Young Women meetings every Sunday and your weekly activities. Learn well your responsibilities in the gospel, and then perform them with diligence.

Regularly attend seminary, and be a seminary

16

graduate. Seminary instruction is one of the most significant spiritual experiences a young woman can have.

Young women, take full advantage of the Church programs. Set your goals to attain excellence in the achievement programs of the Church.

The Personal Progress program for young women is an excellent goal-oriented program. Its purpose is to help you develop the qualities and virtues of exemplary Latter-day Saint young women. Earn the Young Womanhood Recognition Award, and proudly wear the gold medallion. Do not settle for mediocrity in this great incentive program for the young women of the Church.

May I now speak with you about missionary service in the kingdom. I feel very deeply about this. I pray that you will understand the yearnings of my heart.

The Prophet Joseph Smith declared, "After all that has been said, [our] greatest and most important duty is to preach the Gospel." (*History of the Church,* 2:478.)

The Lord wants every young man to serve a full-time mission. Presently only a third of the eligible young men in the Church are serving full-time missions. This is not pleasing to the Lord. We can do better. We *must* do better. Not only should a mission be regarded as a priesthood duty, but every young man should look forward to this experience with great joy and anticipation.

A young man can do nothing more important. School can wait. Scholarships can be deferred. Occupational goals can be postponed. Yes, even temple marriage should wait until after a young man has served an honorable full-time mission for the Lord.

Now, why do I mention this to you young women this evening? Because you can have a positive influence in motivating young men to serve full-time missions. Let the young men of your acquaintance know that you expect them to assume their missionary responsibilities, that you personally want them to serve in the mission field, because you know that's where the Lord wants them.

Avoid steady dating with a young man prior to the time of his mission call. If your relationship with him is more casual, then he can make that decision to serve more easily and also can concentrate his full energies on his missionary work instead of on the girlfriend back home. And after he returns honorably from his mission, he will be a better husband and father and priesthood holder, having first served a full-time mission.

There is no question that faithful Latter-day Saint young women can have a great impact for good in helping young men to magnify their priesthood and to motivate them to good works and to be their best selves.

Remember, young women, you may also have the opportunity to serve a full-time mission. I am grateful my own eternal companion served a mission in Hawaii before we were married in the Salt Lake Temple, and I am pleased that I have had three granddaughters serve full-time missions. Some of our finest missionaries are young sisters.

I would now like to speak to you about personal purity.

Solomon said that the price of a virtuous woman "is far above rubies." (Prov. 31:10.) Young women, guard and protect your virtue as you would your very life. We want you to live the morally clean life all of your life. We want the morally clean life to be your way of life.

Yes, one can repent of moral transgression. The

miracle of forgiveness is real, and true repentance is accepted of the Lord. But it is not pleasing to the Lord to sow one's wild oats, to engage in sexual transgression of any nature, and then expect that planned confession and quick repentance will satisfy the Lord.

President Kimball was emphatic on this point. In his marvelous book *The Miracle of Forgiveness,* he stated:

"That man [or woman] who resists temptation and lives without sin is far better off than the man [or woman] who has fallen, no matter how repentant the latter may be. . . .

"How much better it is never to have committed the sin!" (Salt Lake City: Bookcraft, 1969, 357.)

One of our fine stake presidents shared with us the following experience:

"I remember a girl that I had gone to high school with. She was from a good LDS family, but when she was a junior in high school, she began to compromise her standards and principles.

"I remember how stunned I was one afternoon as a group of us were in the back of the bus, riding home from school, and we were talking about the consequences of sin or transgression. And she flatly announced that she wasn't worried about committing any sin because her bishop had told her she could easily repent and could be quickly forgiven.

"Well, I was shocked with this flippant attitude that didn't reflect any understanding of repentance or appreciation of the miracle of forgiveness. I was also sure that she had grossly misunderstood the instruction and counsel of her bishop."

Adultery, or anything like unto it, is abominable in the sight of the Lord. President Kimball also wisely observed:

"Among the most common sexual sins our young

19

people commit are necking and petting. Not only do these improper relations often lead to fornication, pregnancy, and abortion—all ugly sins—but in and of themselves they are pernicious evils, and it is often difficult for youth to distinguish where one ends and another begins. . . .

"Too often, young people dismiss their petting with a shrug of their shoulders as a *little* indiscretion, while admitting that fornication is a base transgression. Too many of them are shocked, or feign to be, when told that what they have done in the name of petting was in reality [a form of] fornication." (*Miracle of Forgiveness,* 65–66.)

Young sisters, be modest. Modesty in dress and language and deportment is a true mark of refinement and a hallmark of a virtuous Latter-day Saint woman. Shun the low and the vulgar and the suggestive.

Together with the young men of the Aaronic Priesthood, remember the scriptural injunction, "Be ye clean that bear the vessels of the Lord." (3 Ne. 20:41; D&C 38:42; see also Isa. 52:11.)

Remember the story of Joseph in Egypt, who hearkened not to the wife of Potiphar and maintained his purity and virtue. (See Gen. 39:7–21.)

Consider carefully the words of the prophet Alma to his errant son, Corianton, "Forsake your sins, and go no more after the lusts of your eyes." (Alma 39:9.)

"The lusts of your eyes." In our day, what does that expression mean? Movies, television programs, and video recordings that are both suggestive and lewd. Magazines and books that are obscene and pornographic.

We counsel you, young women, not to pollute your minds with such degrading matter, for the mind through which this filth passes is never the same afterward. Don't see R-rated movies or vulgar videos or participate in any entertainment that is immoral, suggestive, or pornographic. And don't accept dates from young men who would take you to such entertainment.

Also, don't listen to music that is degrading. Remember Elder Boyd K. Packer's statement:

"Music, once . . . innocent, now is often used for wicked purposes. . . .

"In our day music itself has been corrupted. Music can, by its tempo, by its beat, by its intensity [and I would add, by its lyrics], dull the spiritual sensitivity of men [and women]. . . .

"Young people," Elder Packer goes on to say, "you cannot afford to fill your mind with the unworthy hard music of our day." ("Inspiring Music — Worthy Thoughts," *Ensign,* January 1974, 25, 28.)

Instead, we encourage you to listen to uplifting music, both popular and classical, that builds the spirit. Learn some favorite hymns from our new hymnbook that build faith and spirituality. Attend dances where the music and the lighting and the dance movements are conducive to the Spirit. Watch those shows and entertainment that lift the spirit and promote clean thoughts and actions. Read books and magazines that do the same.

Remember, young women, the importance of proper dating. President Kimball gave some wise counsel on this subject:

"Clearly, right marriage begins with right dating. . . . Therefore, this warning comes with great emphasis. Do not take the chance of dating nonmembers, or members who are untrained and faithless. A girl may say, 'Oh, I do not intend to marry this person. It is just a "fun" date.' But one cannot afford to take a chance on falling in love with someone who may never accept the gospel." (*Miracle of Forgiveness*, 241–42.)

Our Heavenly Father wants you to date young men who are faithful members of the Church, who will be worthy to take you to the temple and be married the Lord's way. There will be a new spirit in Zion when the young women will say to their boyfriends, "If you cannot get a temple recommend, then I am not about to tie my life to you, even for mortality!" And the young returned missionary will say to his girlfriend, "I am sorry, but as much as I love you, I will not marry out of the holy temple."

My young sisters, we have such hope for you. We have such great expectations for you. Don't settle for less than what the Lord wants you to be.

As the prophet Nephi exclaims in 2 Nephi 31:20: "Wherefore, ye must press forward with a steadfastness in Christ, having a perfect brightness of hope, and a love of God and of all men. Wherefore, if ye shall press forward, feasting upon the word of Christ, and endure to the end, behold, thus sayeth the Father: Ye shall have eternal life."

Yes, give me a young woman who loves home and family, who reads and ponders the scriptures daily, who has a burning testimony of the Book of Mormon. Give me a young woman who faithfully attends her church meetings, who is a seminary graduate, who has earned her Young Womanhood Recognition Award and wears it with pride! Give me a young woman who is virtuous and who has maintained her personal purity, who will not settle for less than a temple marriage, and I will give you a young woman who will perform miracles for the Lord now and throughout eternity.

Now I would like to say a final word to the mothers and to the leaders of these wonderful young women.

Mothers, stay close to your daughters. Earn and deserve their love and respect. Be united with their father in the rearing of your children. Do nothing in your life to cause your daughters to stumble because of your example.

Teach your daughters to prepare for life's greatest career — that of homemaker, wife, and mother. Teach them to love home because you love home. Teach them the importance of being a full-time mother in the home.

My eternal companion has wisely counseled mothers: "Radiate a spirit of contentment and joy with homemaking. You teach by example your attitude toward homemaking. Your attitude will say to your daughters, 'I am only a housewife.' Or it will convey, 'Homemaking is the highest, most noble profession to which a woman might aspire.' "

Priesthood leaders, remember the bishop's first and foremost responsibility is the Aaronic Priesthood and the young women of his ward.

Bishops, stay close to both your young men and young women. Give as much attention to the young women's program in your ward as you do the young men's programs. Be as concerned about the young women's activities and classes, their campouts and socials, their firesides and conferences as you are the young men's.

Recognize with equal prominence the presentation of the Young Womanhood Recognition Award as you do the awarding of the Duty to God Award and Eagle Scout badge.

Spend the necessary time (and it takes time) in personal interviews with the young women of your ward. Talk with them regularly about their goals and aspirations, their challenges and their personal worthiness. Be a bishop who really cares about each of the young men and young women in his ward.

To the Young Women leaders who are here this evening, may you truly love the young sisters with whom you are working. Get inside their lives. Be a true friend and counselor to them. Perform your stewardship well. With all the energy of your heart, help bring them back to our Father in Heaven clean and sweet and pure.

Now, in closing, my dear young sisters, how I love and respect you! How I pray for you! How my hope abounds in you! Remember the counsel I have given you tonight. It is what the Lord would have you hear now—today.

Live up to your divine potential. Remember who you are and the divine heritage that is yours—you are literally the royal daughters of our Father in Heaven. "O youth of the noble birthright," with all my heart I say, "Carry on, carry on, carry on!" (*Hymns,* no. 255), in the name of Jesus Christ, amen.

To the
Mothers in Zion

An address given at a Church-wide
fireside for parents, 22 February 1987

I rejoice in the opportunity of being with you this evening.

I have been touched by the beautiful music and the splendid instructions we have received.

There is no theme I would rather speak to than home and family, for they are at the very heart of the gospel of Jesus Christ. The Church, in large part, exists for the salvation and exaltation of the family.

At a recent general priesthood meeting, I spoke directly to the young men of the Aaronic Priesthood regarding their duties and responsibilities. Shortly thereafter, at a general women's conference, I spoke to the young women of the Church, discussing their opportunities and their sacred callings.

Tonight, at this fireside for parents, seeking the sweet inspiration of heaven, I would like to speak directly to the mothers assembled here and throughout the Church, for you are, or should be, the very heart and soul of the family.

No more sacred word exists in secular or holy writ than that of *mother*. There is no more noble work than that of a good and God-fearing mother.

This evening I pay tribute to the mothers in Zion and pray with all my heart that what I have to say to you will be understood by the Spirit and will lift and bless your lives in your sacred callings as mothers.

President David O. McKay declared: "Motherhood is the greatest potential influence either for good or ill in human life. The mother's image is the first that stamps itself on the unwritten page of the young child's mind. It is her caress that first awakens a sense of security; her kiss, the first realization of affection; her sympathy and tenderness, the first assurance that there is love in the world." (*Gospel Ideals* [Salt Lake City: The Improvement Era, 1953], 452.)

President McKay continues: "Motherhood consists of three principal attributes or qualities: namely, (1) the power to bear, (2) the ability to rear, (3) the gift to love. . . .

"This ability and willingness properly to rear children, the gift to love, and eagerness, yes, longing to express it in soul development, make motherhood the noblest office or calling in the world. She who can paint a masterpiece or write a book that will influence millions deserves the admiration and the plaudits of mankind; but she who rears successfully a family of healthy, beautiful sons and daughters, whose influence will be felt through generations to come, . . . deserves the highest honor that man can give, and the choicest blessings of God." (*Gospel Ideals*, 453–54.)

With all my heart I endorse the words of President McKay.

In the eternal family, God established that fathers are to preside in the home. Fathers are to provide, to love, to teach, and to direct.

But a mother's role is also God-ordained. Mothers are to conceive, to bear, to nourish, to love, and to train. So declare the revelations.

In section 132 of the Doctrine and Covenants, the Lord states that the opportunity and responsibility of wives is "to multiply and replenish the earth, according to my commandment, and to fulfil the promise which was given by my Father before the foundation of the world, and for their exaltation in the eternal worlds, that they may bear the souls of men; for herein is the work of my Father continued, that he may be glorified." (D&C 132:63.)

With this divine injunction, husbands and wives, as co-creators, should eagerly and prayerfully invite children into their homes. Then, as each child joins their family circle, they can gratefully exclaim, as did Hannah, "For this child I prayed; and the Lord hath given me my petition which I asked of him: Therefore also I have lent him to the Lord: as long as he liveth he shall be lent to the Lord." (1 Sam. 1:27–28.)

Isn't that beautiful? A mother praying to bear a child and then giving him to the Lord.

I have always loved the words of Solomon: "Children are an heritage of the Lord: and . . . happy is the man [and woman] that hath [their] quiver full of them." (Ps. 127:3–5.)

I know the special blessings of a large and happy family, for my dear parents had a quiver full of children. Being the oldest of eleven children, I saw the principles of unselfishness, mutual consideration, loyalty to each other, and a host of other virtues developed in a large and wonderful family with my noble mother as the queen of that home.

Young mothers and fathers, with all my heart I counsel you not to postpone having your children, being co-creators with our Father in Heaven.

Do not use the reasoning of the world, such as, "We'll wait until we can better afford having children, until we are more secure, until John has completed his education, until he has a better-paying job, until we have a larger home, until we've obtained a few of the material conveniences," and on and on.

This is the reasoning of the world, and is not pleasing in the sight of God. Mothers who enjoy good health, have your children and have them early. And, husbands, always be considerate of your wives in the bearing of children.

Do not curtail the number of your children for personal or selfish reasons. Material possessions, social convenience, and so-called professional advantages are nothing compared to a righteous posterity. In the eternal perspective, children — not possessions, not position, not prestige — are our greatest jewels.

Brigham Young emphasized: "There are multitudes of pure and holy spirits waiting to take tabernacles, now what is our duty? — To prepare tabernacles for them; to take a course that will not tend to drive those spirits into the families of the wicked, where they will be trained in wickedness, debauchery, and every species of crime. It is the duty of every righteous man and woman to prepare tabernacles for all the spirits they can." (*Discourses of Brigham Young,* sel. John A. Widtsoe [Salt Lake City: Deseret Book Company, 1954], 197.)

Yes, blessed is the husband and wife who have a family of children. The deepest joys and blessings in life are associated with family, parenthood, and sacrifice. To have those sweet spirits come into the home is worth practically any sacrifice.

We realize that some women, through no fault of their own, are not able to bear children. To these lovely sisters, every prophet of God has promised that they will be blessed with children in the eternities and that posterity will not be denied them.

Through pure faith, pleading prayers, fasting, and special priesthood blessings, many of these same lovely sisters, with their noble companions at their sides, have had miracles take place in their lives and have been blessed with children. Others have prayerfully chosen to adopt children, and to these wonderful couples we salute you for the sacrifices and love you have given to those children you have chosen to be your own.

Now, my dear mothers, knowing of your divine role to bear and rear children and bring them back to Him, how will you accomplish this in the Lord's way? I say the "Lord's way," because it is different from the world's way.

The Lord clearly defined the roles of mothers and fathers in providing for and rearing a righteous posterity. In the beginning, Adam—not Eve—was instructed to earn the bread by the sweat of his brow. Contrary to conventional wisdom, a mother's calling is in the home, not in the marketplace.

Again, in the Doctrine and Covenants, we read: "Women have claim on their husbands for their maintenance, until their husbands are taken." (D&C 83:2.)

This is the divine right of a wife and mother. She cares for and nourishes her children at home. Her husband earns the living for the family, which makes this nourishing possible. With that claim on their husbands for their financial support, the counsel of the Church has always been for mothers to spend their full time in the home in rearing and caring for their children.

We realize also that some of our choice sisters are widowed and divorced and that others find themselves in unusual circumstances where, out of necessity, they are required to work for a period of time. But these instances are the exception, not the rule.

In a home where there is an able-bodied husband, he is expected to be the breadwinner. Sometimes we hear of husbands who, because of economic conditions, have lost their jobs and expect their wives to go out of the home and work even though the husband is still capable of providing for his family. In these cases, we urge the husband to do all in his power to allow his wife to remain in the home caring for the children while he continues to provide for his family the best he can, even though the job he is able to secure may not be ideal and family budgeting will have to be tighter.

Our beloved prophet Spencer W. Kimball had much to say about the role of mothers in the home and their callings and responsibilities. I am impressed tonight to share with you some of his inspired pronouncements. I fear that much of his counsel has gone unheeded, and families have suffered because of it. But I stand this evening as a second witness to the truthfulness of what President Spencer W. Kimball said. He spoke as a true prophet of God.

President Kimball declared: "Women are to take care of the family — the Lord has so stated — to be an assistant to the husband, to work with him, but not to earn the living, except in unusual circumstances. Men ought to be men indeed and earn the living under normal circumstances." (*The Teachings of Spencer W. Kimball*, ed. Edward L. Kimball [Salt Lake City: Bookcraft, 1982], 318.)

President Kimball continues: "Too many mothers work away from home to furnish sweaters and music lessons and trips and fun for their children. Too many women spend their time in socializing, in politicking, in public services when they should be home to teach and train and receive and love their children into security." (*Teachings of Spencer W. Kimball*, 319.)

Remember the counsel of President Kimball to John and Mary: "Mary, you are to become a career woman in the greatest career on earth — that of homemaker, wife, and mother. It was never intended by the Lord that married women should compete with

30

men in employment. They have a far greater and more important service to render." (*Faith Precedes the Miracle* [Salt Lake City: Deseret Book Company, 1972], 128.)

Again President Kimball speaks: "The husband is expected to support his family and only in an emergency should a wife secure outside employment. Her place is in the home, to build the home into a heaven of delight.

"Numerous divorces can be traced directly to the day when the wife left the home and went out into the world into employment. Two incomes raise the standard of living beyond its norm. Two spouses working prevent the complete and proper home life, break into the family prayers, create an independence which is not cooperative, causes distortion, limits the family, and frustrates the children already born." (Fireside address, San Antonio, Texas, 3 Dec. 1977.)

Finally, President Kimball counsels: "I beg of you, you who could and should be bearing and rearing a family: wives, come home from the typewriter, the laundry, the nursing, come home from the factory, the cafe. No career approaches in importance that of wife, homemaker, mother—cooking meals, washing dishes, making beds for one's precious husband and children. Come home, wives, to your husbands. Make home a heaven for them. Come home, wives, to your children, born and unborn. Wrap the motherly cloak about you and, unembarrassed, help in a major role to create the bodies for the immortal souls who anxiously await.

"When you have fully complemented your husband in home life and borne the children, growing up full of faith, integrity, responsibility, and goodness, then you have achieved your accomplishment supreme, without peer, and you will be the envy [of all] through time and eternity." (Fireside address, San Antonio, Texas.)

President Kimball spoke the truth. His words are prophetic.

Mothers in Zion, your God-given roles are so vital to your own exaltation and to the salvation and exaltation of your family. A child needs a mother more than all the things money can buy. Spending time with your children is the greatest gift of all.

With love in my heart for the mothers in Zion, I would now like to suggest ten specific ways our mothers may spend effective time with their children.

Be at the Crossroads. First, take time to always be at the crossroads when your children are either coming or going—when they leave and return from school, when they leave and return from dates, when they bring friends home. Be there at the crossroads whether your children are six or sixteen. In Proverbs we read, "A child left to himself bringeth his mother to shame." (Prov. 29:15.) Among the greatest concerns in our society are the millions of latchkey children who come home daily to empty houses, unsupervised by working parents.

Be a Real Friend. Second, mothers, take time to be a real friend to your children. Listen to your children, really listen. Talk with them, laugh and joke with them, sing with them, play with them, cry with them, hug them, honestly praise them. Yes, regularly spend unrushed one-on-one time with each child. Be a real friend to your children.

Read to Your Children. Third, mothers, take time to read to your children. Starting from the cradle, read to your sons and daughters. Remember what the poet said:

> You may have tangible wealth untold;
> Caskets of jewels and coffers of gold.
> Richer than I you can never be—

I had a mother who read to me.
(Strickland Gillilan, "The Reading Mother.")

You will plant a love for good literature and a real love for the scriptures if you will read to your children regularly.

Pray with Your Children. Fourth, take time to pray with your children. Family prayers, under the direction of the father, should be held morning and night. Have your children feel of your faith as you call down the blessings of heaven upon them. Paraphrasing the words of James, "The . . . fervent prayer of a righteous [mother] availeth much." (James 5:16.) Have your children participate in family and personal prayers, and rejoice in their sweet utterances to their Father in Heaven.

Have Weekly Home Evenings. Fifth, take time to have a meaningful weekly home evening. With your husband presiding, participate in a spiritual and an uplifting home evening each week. Have your children actively involved. Teach them correct principles. Make this one of your great family traditions. Remember the marvelous promise made by President Joseph F. Smith when home evenings were first introduced to the Church: "If the Saints obey this counsel, we promise that great blessings will result. Love at home and obedience to parents will increase. Faith will be developed in the hearts of the youth of Israel, and they will gain power to combat the evil influence and temptations which beset them." (James R. Clark, comp., *Messages of the First Presidency of The Church of Jesus Christ of Latter-day Saints,* 6 vols. [Salt Lake City: Bookcraft, 1965–75], 4:339.) This wonderful promise is still in effect today.

Be Together at Mealtimes. Sixth, take time to be together at mealtimes as often as possible. This is a

33

challenge as the children get older and lives get busier. But happy conversation, sharing of the day's plans and activities, and special teaching moments occur at mealtime because mothers and fathers and children work at it.

Read Scriptures Daily. Seventh, take time daily to read the scriptures together as a family. Individual scripture reading is important, but family scripture reading is vital. Reading the Book of Mormon together as a family will especially bring increased spirituality into your home and will give both parents and children the power to resist temptation and to have the Holy Ghost as their constant companion. I promise you that the Book of Mormon will change the lives of your family.

Do Things as a Family. Eighth, take time to do things together as a family. Make family outings and picnics and birthday celebrations and trips special times and memory builders. Whenever possible, attend, as a family, events where one of the family members is involved, such as a school play, a ball game, a talk, a recital. Attend church meetings together and sit together as a family when you can. Mothers who help families pray and play together will stay together and will bless children's lives forever.

Teach Your Children. Ninth, mothers, take time to teach your children. Catch the teaching moments. This can be done anytime during the day—at mealtimes, in casual settings, or at special sit-down times together, at the foot of the bed at the end of the day, or during an early morning walk together. Mothers, you are your children's best teacher. Don't shift this precious responsibility to day-care centers or baby-sitters. A mother's love and prayerful concern for her children are her most important ingredients in teaching her own.

Teach children gospel principles. Teach them it pays to be good. Teach them there is no safety in sin. Teach them a love for the gospel of Jesus Christ and a testimony of its divinity.

Teach your sons and daughters modesty, and teach them to respect manhood and womanhood. Teach your children sexual purity, proper dating standards, temple marriage, missionary service, and the importance of accepting and magnifying Church callings.

Teach them a love for work and the value of a good education.

Teach them the importance of the right kind of entertainment, including appropriate movies and videos and music and books and magazines. Discuss the evils of pornography and drugs, and teach them the value of living the clean life.

Yes, mothers, teach your children the gospel in your own home, at your own fireside. This is the most effective teaching that your children will ever receive. This is the Lord's way of teaching. The Church cannot teach like you can. The school cannot. The day-care center cannot. But you can, and the Lord will sustain you. Your children will remember your teachings forever, and when they are old, they will not depart from them. (See Prov. 22:6.) They will call you blessed— their truly angel mother.

Mothers, this kind of heavenly, motherly teaching takes time—lots of time. It cannot be done effectively part-time. It must be done all the time in order to save and exalt your children. This is your divine calling.

Truly Love Your Children. Tenth and finally, mothers, take the time to truly love your children. A mother's unqualified love approaches Christlike love.

Here is a beautiful tribute by a son to his mother: "I don't remember much about her views of voting nor her social prestige; and what her ideas on child training, diet, and eugenics were, I cannot recall. The main thing that sifts back to me now through the thick undergrowth of years is that she loved me. She liked to lie on the grass with me and tell stories, or to run and hide with us children. She was always hugging me. And I liked it. She had a sunny face. To me it was like God, and all the beatitudes saints tell of Him. And sing! Of all the sensations pleasurable to my life nothing can compare with the rapture of crawling up into her lap and going to sleep while she swung to and fro in her rocking chair and sang. Thinking of this, I wonder if the woman of today, with all her tremendous notions and plans, realizes what an almighty factor she is in shaping of her child for weal or woe. I wonder if she realizes how much sheer love and attention count for in a child's life."

Mothers, your teenage children also need that same kind of love and attention. It seems easier for many mothers and fathers to express and show their love to their children when they are young, but more difficult when they are older. Work at this prayerfully. There need be no generation gap. And the key is love. Our young people need love and attention, not indulgence. They need empathy and understanding, not indifference from mothers and fathers. They need the parents' time. A mother's kindly teachings and her love for and confidence in a teenage son or daughter can literally save them from a wicked world.

In closing, I would be remiss this evening if I did not express my love and eternal gratitude for my sweetheart and companion and the mother of our six children. Her devotion to motherhood has blessed me and our family beyond words of expression. She has been a marvelous mother, completely and happily

36

devoting her life and her mission to her family. How grateful I am for Flora!

May I also express my gratitude to you fathers and husbands assembled this evening. We look to you to give righteous leadership in your home and families and, with your companions and the mothers of your children, to lead your families back to our Eternal Father.

Now God bless our wonderful mothers. We pray for you. We sustain you. We honor you as you bear, nourish, train, teach, and love for eternity. I promise you the blessings of heaven and "all that [the] Father hath" (see D&C 84:38) as you magnify the noblest calling of all—a mother in Zion. In the name of Jesus Christ, amen.

To the
Fathers in Israel

*An address given at the priesthood
session of general conference, 3 October 1987*

My dear brethren, I am grateful to be here with you in this glorious assembly of the priesthood of God. I pray that the Spirit of the Lord will be with me and with you as I address you on a most vital subject. This evening I would like to speak to the fathers assembled here and throughout the Church about their sacred callings.

I hope you young men will also listen carefully, inasmuch as you are now preparing to become the future fathers of the Church.

Fathers, yours is an eternal calling from which you are never released. Callings in the Church, as important as they are, by their very nature are only for a period of time, and then an appropriate release takes place. But a father's calling is eternal, and its importance transcends time. It is a calling for both time and eternity.

President Harold B. Lee truly stated that "the most important of the Lord's work that you [fathers] will ever do will be the work you do within the walls of your own home. Home Teaching, bishopric's work, and other Church duties are all important, but the most important work is within the walls of your home." (*Decisions for Successful Living* [Salt Lake City: Deseret Book Company, 1973], 248–49.)

What, then, is a father's specific responsibility

39

within the sacred walls of his home? May I suggest two basic responsibilities of every father in Israel.

First, you have a sacred responsibility to provide for the material needs of your family.

The Lord clearly defined the roles of providing for and rearing a righteous posterity. In the beginning, Adam, not Eve, was instructed to earn the bread by the sweat of his brow.

The Apostle Paul counsels husbands and fathers, "But if any provide not for his own, and specially for those of his own house, he hath denied the faith, and is worse than an infidel." (1 Tim. 5:8.)

Early in the history of the restored Church, the Lord specifically charged men with the obligation to provide for their wives and family. In January of 1832 He said, "Verily I say unto you, that every man who is obliged to provide for his own family, let him provide, and he shall in nowise lose his crown." (D&C 75:28.) Three months later the Lord said again, "Women have claim on their husbands for their maintenance, until their husbands are taken." (D&C 83:2.) This is the divine right of a wife and mother. While she cares for and nourishes her children at home, her husband earns the living for the family, which makes this nourishing possible.

In a home where there is an able-bodied husband, he is expected to be the breadwinner. Sometimes we hear of husbands who, because of economic conditions, have lost their jobs and expect the wives to go out of the home and work, even though the husband is still capable of providing for his family. In these cases, we urge the husband to do all in his power to allow his wife to remain in the home caring for the children while he continues to provide for his family the best he can, even though the job he is able to secure may not be ideal and family budgeting may have to be tighter.

Also, the need for education or material things does not justify the postponing of children in order to keep the wife working as the breadwinner of the family.

I remember the counsel of our beloved prophet Spencer W. Kimball to married students. He said: "I have told tens of thousands of young folks that when they marry they should not wait for children until they have finished their schooling and financial desires. . . . They should live together normally and let the children come. . . .

"I know of no scriptures," President Kimball continued, "where an authorization is given to young wives to withhold their families and to go to work to put their husbands through school. There are thousands of husbands who have worked their own way through school and have reared families at the same time." ("Marriage Is Honorable," in *Speeches of the Year, 1973* [Provo: Brigham Young University Press, 1974], 263.)

Brethren of the priesthood, I continue to emphasize the importance of mothers staying home to nurture, care for, and train their children in the principles of righteousness.

As I travel throughout the Church, I feel that the great majority of Latter-day Saint mothers earnestly want to follow this counsel. But we know that sometimes the mother works outside of the home at the encouragement, or even insistence, of her husband. It is he who wants the items of convenience that the extra income can buy. Not only will the family suffer in such instances, brethren, but your own spiritual growth and progression will be hampered. I say to all of you, the Lord has charged men with the responsibility to provide for their families in such a way that the wife is allowed to fulfill her role as mother in the home.

Fathers, another vital aspect of providing for the material needs of your family is the provision you should be making for your family in case of an emergency. Family preparedness has been a long-established welfare principle. It is even more urgent today. I ask you earnestly, have you provided for your family a year's supply of food, clothing, and, where possible, fuel? The revelation to produce and store food may be as essential to our temporal welfare today as boarding the ark was to the people in the days of Noah.

Also, are you living within your income and saving a little?

Are you honest with the Lord in the payment of your tithes? Living this divine law will bring both spiritual and material blessings.

Yes, brethren, as fathers in Israel you have a great responsibility to provide for the material needs of your family and to have the necessary provisions in case of emergency.

Second, you have a sacred responsibility to provide spiritual leadership in your family.

In a pamphlet published some years ago by the Council of the Twelve, we said the following: "Fatherhood is leadership, the most important kind of leadership. It has always been so; it always will be so. Father, with the assistance and counsel and encouragement of your eternal companion, you preside in the home." (*Father, Consider Your Ways* [Salt Lake City: The Church of Jesus Christ of Latter-day Saints, 1973], 4–5.

However, along with that presiding position come important obligations. We sometimes hear accounts

42

of men, even in the Church, who think that being head of the home somehow puts them in a superior role and allows them to dictate and make demands upon their family.

The Apostle Paul points out that "the husband is the head of the wife, *even as* Christ is the head of the church." (Eph. 5:23; italics added.) That is the model we are to follow in our role of presiding in the home. We do not find the Savior leading the Church with a harsh or unkind hand. We do not find the Savior treating His Church with disrespect or neglect. We do not find the Savior using force or coercion to accomplish His purposes. Nowhere do we find the Savior doing anything but that which edifies, uplifts, comforts, and exalts the Church. Brethren, I say to you with all soberness, He is the model we must follow as we take the spiritual lead in our families.

Particularly is this true in your relationship with your wife.

Here again the counsel from the Apostle Paul is most beautiful and to the point. He said simply, "Husbands, love your wives, even as Christ also loved the church." (Eph. 5:25.)

In latter-day revelation the Lord speaks again of this obligation. He said, "Thou shalt love thy wife with all thy heart, and shalt cleave unto her and none else." (D&C 42:22.) To my knowledge there is only one other thing in all scripture that we are commanded to love with all our hearts, and that is God Himself. Think what that means!

This kind of love can be shown for your wives in so many ways. First and foremost, nothing except God Himself takes priority over your wife in your life— not work, not recreation, not hobbies. Your wife is your precious, eternal helpmate—your companion.

43

What does it mean to love someone with all your heart? It means to love with all your emotional feelings and with all your devotion. Surely, when you love your wife with all your heart, you cannot demean her, criticize her, find fault with her, or abuse her by words, sullen behavior, or actions.

What does it mean to "cleave unto her"? It means to stay close to her, to be loyal and faithful to her, to communicate with her, and to express your love for her.

Love means being sensitive to her feelings and needs. She wants to be noticed and treasured. She wants to be told that you view her as lovely and attractive and important to you. Love means putting her welfare and self-esteem as a high priority in your life.

You should be grateful that she is the mother of your children and the queen of your home, grateful that she has chosen homemaking and motherhood— to bear, to nourish, to love, and to train your children—as the noblest calling of all.

Husbands, recognize your wife's intelligence and her ability to counsel with you as a real partner regarding family plans, family activities, and family budgeting. Don't be stingy with your time or with your means. Give her the opportunity to grow intellectually, emotionally, and socially as well as spiritually.

Remember, brethren, love can be nurtured and nourished by little tokens. Flowers on special occasions are wonderful, but so is your willingness to help with the dishes, change diapers, get up with a crying child in the night, and leave the television or the newspaper to help with the dinner. Those are the quiet ways we say "I love you" with our actions. They bring rich dividends for such little effort.

This kind of loving priesthood leadership applies to your children as well as to your wife.

Mothers play an important role as the heart of the home, but this in no way lessens the equally important role fathers should play, as head of the home, in nurturing, training, and loving their children.

As the patriarch in your home, you have a serious responsibility to assume leadership in working with your children. You must help create a home where the Spirit of the Lord can abide. Your place is to give direction to all family life. You should take an active part in establishing family rules and discipline.

Your homes should be havens of peace and joy for your family. Surely no child should fear his own father — especially a priesthood father. A father's duty is to make his home a place of happiness and joy. He cannot do this when there is bickering, quarreling, contention, or unrighteous behavior. The powerful effect of righteous fathers in setting an example, disciplining and training, nurturing and loving is vital to the spiritual welfare of his children.

With love in my heart for the fathers in Israel, may I suggest ten specific ways that fathers can give spiritual leadership to their children:

1. Give father's blessings to your children. Baptize and confirm your children. Ordain your sons to the priesthood. These will become spiritual highlights in the lives of your children.

2. Personally direct family prayers, daily scripture reading, and weekly family home evenings. Your personal involvement will show your children how important these activities really are.

3. Whenever possible, attend Church meetings together as a family. Family worship under your leadership is vital to your children's spiritual welfare.

4. Go on daddy-daughter dates and father-and-

sons' outings with your children. As a family, go on campouts and picnics, to ball games and recitals, to school programs, and so forth. Having Dad there makes all the difference.

5. Build traditions of family vacations and trips and outings. These memories will never be forgotten by your children.

6. Have regular one-on-one visits with your children. Let them talk about what they would like to. Teach them gospel principles. Teach them true values. Tell them you love them. Personal time with your children tells them where Dad puts his priorities.

7. Teach your children to work, and show them the value of working toward a worthy goal. Establishing mission funds and education funds for your children shows them what Dad considers to be important.

8. Encourage good music and art and literature in your homes. Homes that have a spirit of refinement and beauty will bless the lives of your children forever.

9. As distances allow, regularly attend the temple with your wife. Your children will then better understand the importance of temple marriage and temple vows and the eternal family unit.

10. Have your children see your joy and satisfaction in service to the Church. This can become contagious to them, so they, too, will want to serve in the Church and will love the kingdom.

Oh, husbands and fathers in Israel, you can do so much for the salvation and exaltation of your families! Your responsibilities are so important.

Remember your sacred calling as a father in Israel—your most important calling in time and eternity—a calling from which you will never be released.

May you always provide for the material needs of

your family and, with your eternal companion at your side, may you fulfill your sacred responsibility to provide the spiritual leadership in your home.

To this end I pray, in the name of Jesus Christ, amen.

To the
Single Adult Brethren
of the Church

*An address given at the priesthood
session of general conference, 2 April 1988*

My dear brethren of the Aaronic and Melchizedek Priesthood, how happy I am to be with you this evening.

I rejoice in the messages of my Brethren who have preceded me, and I now ask you for your faith and prayers in my behalf as I address you.

For some time I have wanted to speak directly to the great body of single adult brethren of the Church. Many of you have served full-time missions. Many of you are giving outstanding service in your wards and stakes.

To you single adult brethren, I want you to know of my great love for each of you. I have great expectations for you and a great hope in you. You have so much to contribute to the Lord and to the kingdom of God now and in the future. You may be twenty-seven years of age, or thirty, or possibly even older.

Just what are your priorities at this time in your life?

May I suggest for your careful consideration the counsel we give to returning missionaries. This counsel applies just as much to those who have been home for a while as to those who may not have served full-time missions for the Church.

Here are some of the priorities we pray that you

single adult brethren will consider to be essential in your life.

First, continue to draw close to the Savior through private, sincere, heartfelt prayer. Remember always that "the effectual fervent prayer of a righteous man availeth much." (James 5:16.)

"Feast upon the words of Christ" (2 Ne. 32:3) by consistently studying the scriptures every day and by following the counsel of the living prophets. Particularly make the study of the Book of Mormon a lifetime pursuit and daily sup from its pages.

Be an example in your Church activity—honor the Sabbath day, attend your meetings, observe the Word of Wisdom, pay your tithes and offerings, support your leaders, and otherwise keep the commandments. Serve cheerfully and gratefully in every calling you receive. Live worthy of a temple recommend and enjoy the sweet, sacred spirit that comes from frequent temple attendance.

Dress and groom yourself in a way that reflects your lifelong commitment to share the gospel with others.

Be thoughtful, loving, helpful, and appreciative of your family as you seek to deepen those eternal relationships.

In your dating and courting, fully maintain the standards of the Church. Be morally clean. "Let virtue garnish [your] thoughts unceasingly." (D&C 121:45.)

Remember the counsel of Elder Bruce R. McConkie that "the most important single thing that any Latter-day Saint ever does in this world is to marry the *right* person in the *right* place by the *right* authority." (*Choose an Eternal Companion,* Brigham Young University Speeches of the Year, 3 May 1966 [Provo: Brigham Young University Press, 1966], 2.)

Understand that temple marriage is essential to your salvation and exaltation.

Carefully select practical and worthwhile goals and, in an organized way, work to reach them.

Apply yourself prayerfully and diligently to selecting and pursuing academic and vocational goals.

Share the gospel and your testimony with those who are not members of the Church or who are less active.

Improve your community by active participation and service. Remember in your civic responsibility that "the only thing necessary for the triumph of evil is for good men to do nothing." (Edmund Burke, in *The Great Thoughts,* comp. George Seldes [New York: Ballantine Books, 1985], 60.) Do something meaningful in defense of your God-given freedom and liberty.

Remember that your entire life is a mission and that each new phase of it can be richly rewarding as you magnify your talents and take advantage of your opportunities.

May I now say an additional word about an eternal opportunity and responsibility to which I have referred earlier and which is of greatest importance to you. I am referring to celestial marriage.

Just a few weeks ago, I received a letter from two devoted parents, part of which reads as follows:

"Dear President Benson: We are concerned about what seems to be a growing problem—at least in this part of the Church familiar to us—that is, so many choice young men in the Church over the age of thirty who are still unmarried.

"We have sons thirty, thirty-one, and thirty-three in this situation. Many of our friends also are experiencing this same concern for unmarried sons and daughters."

Their letter continues:

"In our experience these are usually young men who have been on missions, are well educated, and are living the commandments (except this most important one). There does not appear to be a lack of choice young ladies in the same age bracket who could make suitable companions.

"It is most frustrating to us, as their parents, who sometimes feel we have failed in our parental teachings and guiding responsibilities."

My dear single adult brethren, *we* are also concerned. We want you to know that the position of the Church has never changed regarding the importance of celestial marriage. It is a commandment of God. The Lord's declaration in Genesis is still true: "And the Lord God said, It is not good that the man should be alone." (Gen. 2:18.)

To obtain a fulness of glory and exaltation in the celestial kingdom, one must enter into this holiest of ordinances.

Without marriage, the purposes of the Lord would be frustrated. Choice spirits would be withheld from the experience of mortality. And postponing marriage unduly often means limiting your posterity, and the time will come, brethren, when you will feel and know that loss.

I can assure you that the greatest responsibility and the greatest joys in life are centered in the family, honorable marriage, and rearing a righteous posterity. And the older you become, the less likely you are to marry, and then you may lose these eternal blessings altogether.

President Spencer W. Kimball recounted an experience he once had:

"Recently I met a young returned missionary who is 35 years old. He had been home from his mission for 14 years and yet he was little concerned about his bachelorhood, and laughed about it.

"I shall feel sorry for this young man when the day comes that he faces the Great Judge at the throne and when the Lord asks this boy: 'Where is your wife?' All of his excuses which he gave to his fellows on earth will seem very light and senseless when he answers the Judge. 'I was very busy,' or 'I felt I should get my education first,' or 'I did not find the right girl'—such answers will be hollow and of little avail. He knew he was commanded to find a wife and marry her and make her happy. He knew it was his duty to become the father of children and provide a rich, full life for them as they grew up. He knew all this, yet postponed his responsibility." ("The Marriage Decision," *Ensign*, Feb. 1975, 2.)

I realize that some of you brethren may have genuine fears regarding the real responsibilities that will be yours if you do marry. You are concerned about being able to support a wife and family and provide them with the necessities in these uncertain economic times. Those fears must be replaced with faith.

I assure you, brethren, that if you will be industrious, faithfully pay your tithes and offerings, and conscientiously keep the commandments, the Lord will sustain you. Yes, there will be sacrifices required, but you will grow from these and will be a better man for having met them.

Work hard educationally and in your vocation. Put your trust in the Lord, have faith, and it will work out. The Lord never gives a commandment without providing the means to accomplish it. (See 1 Ne. 3:7.)

Also, do not be caught up in materialism, one of the real plagues of our generation—that is, acquiring things, fast-paced living, and securing career success in the single state.

Honorable marriage is more important than wealth, position, and status. As husband and wife, you can achieve your life's goals together. As you sacrifice for each other and your children, the Lord will bless you, and your commitment to the Lord and your service in His kingdom will be enhanced.

Now, brethren, do not expect perfection in your choice of a mate. Do not be so particular that you overlook her most important qualities of having a strong testimony, living the principles of the gospel, loving home, wanting to be a mother in Zion, and supporting you in your priesthood responsibilities.

Of course, she should be attractive to you, but do not just date one girl after another for the sole pleasure of dating without seeking the Lord's confirmation in your choice of your eternal companion.

And one good yardstick as to whether a person might be the right one for you is this: in her presence, do you think your noblest thoughts, do you aspire to your finest deeds, do you wish you were better than you are?

God bless you single adult brethren of the Church. May your priorities be right. I have suggested some very important priorities this evening. May you seriously consider and ponder them.

Know, my good brethren, that I have spoken from my heart and by His Spirit because of my love and concern for you. It is what the Lord would have you hear today. With all my heart I echo the words of the prophet Lehi from the Book of Mormon, "Arise from the dust, my sons, and be men" (2 Ne. 1:21), in the name of Jesus Christ, amen.

To the
Single Adult Sisters
of the Church

*An address given at the general women's
meeting of the Church, 24 September 1988*

My dear sisters, it's so good to be with you. This
has been a glorious meeting. I have appreciated the
counsel we have received from the presidents of these
three great women's organizations. Their words have
been inspiring, and I commend them to you.

The music has been beautiful, especially this last
anthem—"Come, Hold Your Torches High"—"That
Christ's true light through us will shine, . . . his name
to glorify." (Carolyn J. Rasmus and Larry W. Bastian,
"Come, Hold Your Torches High" [Salt Lake City:
The Church of Jesus Christ of Latter-day Saints,
1988].) May that be the clarion call for each of us as
we serve in God's kingdom.

Six months ago I spoke at this pulpit in general
priesthood meeting to the single adult brethren of the
Church. This evening I would like to speak for a few
minutes to the single adult sisters of the Church.

Single adult sisters throughout the Church, I want
you to know of my deep love and appreciation for
you—for your goodness, for your faithfulness, for
your desire to serve the Lord with all your heart "that
Christ's true light through [you] will shine, . . . his
name to glorify."

We see so many of you living Christlike lives worthy of emulation and giving such dedicated service in
the Church.

We see you leading the music in Primary and, because of your love and care, children's eyes lighting up as they sing the sweet songs of Zion.

We see you teaching by the Spirit classes in Relief Society, Young Women, Primary, and Sunday School with such excellent preparation and bearing testimony of gospel truths and touching others' lives.

We see many of you effectively working with our teenage girls, taking them to camp, directing road-shows, going to their dances, and being a great example and a real friend to them.

We see you serving full-time missions for the Lord with devotion and dedication and returning from the mission field with an even greater capacity to serve.

We see you in singles wards and resident wards reaching out to the less active, to the shy, to the troubled, reaching out to the widow, the shut-in, and the lonely and inviting all of them to come unto Christ.

We see wise bishops and stake presidents calling you single adult sisters to leadership responsibilities in wards and stakes. We see you in the presidencies of Relief Society, Young Women, and Primary organizations, where your talents and abilities are being fully utilized.

We see you as a vital part of the mainstream body of the Church. We pray that the emphasis we naturally place on families will not make you feel less needed or less valuable to the Lord or to His Church. The sacred bonds of Church membership go far beyond marital status, age, or present circumstance. Your individual worth as a daughter of God transcends all.

Now, we also know you have special challenges and special needs. Be assured that we are aware of these.

I would like to express the hope we all have for you, which is so real, that you will be exalted in the highest degree of glory in the celestial kingdom and that you will enter into the new and everlasting covenant of marriage.

Dear sisters, never lose sight of this sacred goal. Prayerfully prepare for it and live for it. Be married the Lord's way. Temple marriage is a gospel ordinance of exaltation. Our Father in Heaven wants each of His daughters to have this eternal blessing.

Therefore, don't trifle away your happiness by involvement with someone who cannot take you worthily to the temple. Make a decision now that this is the place where you will marry. To leave that decision until a romantic involvement develops is to take a risk the importance of which you cannot now fully calculate.

And remember, you are not required to lower your standards in order to get a mate. Keep yourselves attractive, maintain high standards, maintain your self-respect. Do not engage in intimacies that bring heartache and sorrow. Place yourselves in a position to meet worthy men and be engaged in constructive activities

But also, do not expect perfection in your choice of a mate. Do not be so concerned about his physical appearance and his bank account that you overlook his more important qualities. Of course, he should be attractive to you, and he should be able to financially provide for you. But, does he have a strong testimony? Does he live the principles of the gospel and magnify his priesthood? Is he active in his ward and stake? Does he love home and family, and will he be a faithful husband and a good father? *These* are qualities that really matter.

And I would also caution you single sisters not to become so independent and self-reliant that you decide marriage isn't worth it and you can do just as well on your own. Some of our sisters indicate that they do not want to consider marriage until *after* they have completed their degrees or pursued a career. This is not right. Certainly we want our single sisters to maximize their individual potential, to be well educated, and to do well at their present employment. You have much to contribute to society, to your community, and to your neighborhood. But we earnestly pray that our single sisters will desire honorable marriage in the temple to a worthy man and rear a righteous family, even though this may mean the sacrificing of degrees and careers. Our priorities are right when we realize there is no higher calling than to be an honorable wife and mother.

I also recognize that not all women in the Church will have an opportunity for marriage and motherhood in mortality. But if those of you in this situation are worthy and endure faithfully, you can be assured of all blessings from a kind and loving Heavenly Father—and I emphasize *all blessings.*

I assure you that if you have to wait even until the next life to be blessed with a choice companion, God will surely compensate you. Time is numbered only to man. God has your eternal perspective in mind.

I also recognize that some of our sisters are widowed or divorced. My heart is drawn to you who are in these circumstances. The Brethren pray for you, and we feel a great obligation to see that your needs are met. Trust in the Lord. Be assured He loves you and we love you.

If you are a single parent, make friends with others in similar situations and develop friendships with married couples. Counsel with your priesthood leaders. Let them know of your needs and wants. Single parenthood is understood by the Lord. He knows the special challenges that are yours. You are His daughters. He loves you and will bless and sustain you. This I know.

Now, to *all* the single adult sisters, regardless of your present situations:

Be faithful. Keep the commandments. Establish a deep and abiding relationship with the Lord Jesus Christ. Know that He is there—always there. Reach out to Him. He does answer prayers. He does bring peace. He does give hope. In the words of the Psalmist: "He is my refuge and my fortress: . . . in him will I trust." (Ps. 91:2.) Study carefully the life of the Savior. He is our great exemplar.

Make the scriptures your constant companion. Read daily from the Book of Mormon and receive of its strength and spiritual power.

Realize your personal self-worth. Never demean yourself. Realize the strength of your inner self and that, with God's help, you "can do all things through Christ which strengtheneth [you]." (Philip. 4:1.) Life does not begin only upon marriage. There are important things for you to do right now.

Sister Eliza R. Snow declared: "There is no sister so isolated, and her sphere so narrow but what she can do a great deal towards establishing the kingdom of God upon the earth." ("An Address," *Woman's Exponent*, 15 Sep. 1873, 62.)

Become fully involved in the Church. Attend all your meetings and your single adult activities.

Reach out to others. Rather than turning inward, forget self and really serve others in your Church callings, in personal deeds of compassionate service, in unknown, unheralded personal acts of kindness.

If you really want to receive joy and happiness, then serve others with all your heart. Lift their burdens, and your own burdens will be lighter. Truly in the words of Jesus of Nazareth: "He that findeth his life shall lose it: and he that loseth his life for my sake shall find it." (Matt. 10:39.)

And always be improving yourselves. Set personal achievement goals and stretch to accomplish them. Improve yourselves physically, socially, mentally, and spiritually. Incorporate the splendid Pursuit of Excellence program into your life. Keep growing and learning and progressing and serving others.

And finally, my dear sisters, be thankful to the Lord for your blessings. Think more about what you *do* have than what you *don't* have. Dwell upon the goodnesses of the Lord to you. Remember His words to the Prophet Joseph: "He who receiveth all things with thankfulness shall be made glorious; and the things of this earth shall be added unto him, even an hundred fold, yea, more." (D&C 78:19.)

My humble desire for the wonderful single adult sisters of the Church is that you will receive all that the Father hath, "even an hundred fold, yea, more."

And I promise you that indeed you will. All of the blessings of our Father in Heaven will be yours if you continue faithful, if you are true, and if you serve Him and His children with all your heart, might, mind, and strength.

You are choice daughters of our Father in Heaven. You are jewels in His crown. Your virtue and purity make your price above rubies.

In the words of President David O. McKay, "A beautiful, modest, gracious woman is creation's masterpiece. When to these virtues a woman possesses as guiding stars in her life righteousness and godliness and an irresistible impulse and desire to make others happy, no one will question if she be classed among those who are the truly great." (*Gospel Ideals: Selections from the Discourses of David O. McKay* [Salt Lake City: The Improvement Era, 1953], 449.)

God bless and sustain you always. I leave my blessings upon you wonderful sisters with love in my heart for you, and do so in the name of Jesus Christ, amen.

To the Children
of the Church

*An address given at the Sunday afternoon
session of general conference, 2 April 1989*

My dear brethren and sisters, how I have rejoiced in the messages I have heard delivered from this pulpit at this great general conference of the Church

The messages are true. They are important. They are vital to our personal salvation, and with all my heart I commend them to you.

In previous general meetings of the Church, I have spoken specifically to the mothers and to the fathers, to the young men and to the young women, to the single adult sisters and to the single adult brethren.

For my closing message at this conference, I would now like to speak to the children of the Church—yes, to *you*, our precious children. And as you listen, I pray that you will know that this is a personal message just for you.

How I love you! How our Heavenly Father loves you!

Just like the beautiful Primary song you sing, each of you truly *is* a child of God. For you, rich blessings *are* in store, and if you learn to do His will, you *will* live with Him once more. I know this to be true. (See "I Am a Child of God," in *Hymns of The Church of Jesus Christ of Latter-day Saints* [Salt Lake City: The Church of Jesus Christ of Latter-day Saints, 1985], no. 301.)

Today I desire to teach you what our Heavenly Father wants you to know so that you can learn to do His will and enjoy true happiness. It will help you now and throughout your life.

First, may I say how thrilled I am to know how you children are learning about the Book of Mormon. This is one of the very important things Heavenly Father wants you to do.

I know you are reading the Book of Mormon, for I have received hundreds of personal letters from you telling me that you are reading this sacred book. It makes me weep for joy when I hear this.

Many of you have read the Book of Mormon all the way through. In family home evening and in Primary you have dramatized Book of Mormon stories, you have sung songs about the Book of Mormon, you have learned the names of the books in the Book of Mormon, you have played Book of Mormon games, you have learned about wonderful Book of Mormon prophets. Some of you have even earned money to send copies of the Book of Mormon around the world.

How pleased I am to hear of your love for the Book of Mormon. *I* love it too, and Heavenly Father wants you to continue to learn from the Book of Mormon every day. It's Heavenly Father's special gift to you. By following its teachings, you will learn to do the will of our Father in Heaven.

I also hope your parents and leaders will give you opportunities to learn from the Doctrine and Covenants, the Pearl of Great Price, and the Bible as well.

Now, there are other important things Heavenly Father wants you to do.

He wants you to pray to Him every day. He wants to help you because He loves you, and He *will* help you if you pray to Him and ask Him for His help. In your prayers also thank Him for your blessings. Thank Him for sending our oldest brother, Jesus Christ, into the world. He made it possible for us to return to our heavenly home. Thank Him for your family. Thank Him for the Church. Thank Him for this beautiful world you live in. Ask Him to protect you. In your prayers, ask Him to help you know what to do in your life. When you make mistakes, your Heavenly Father still loves you. So pray to Him, and He will help you try again to do right.

Pray to Heavenly Father to bless you with His Spirit at all times. We often call the Spirit the Holy Ghost. The Holy Ghost is also a gift from Heavenly Father. The Holy Ghost helps you to choose the right. The Holy Ghost will protect you from evil. He whispers to you in a still, small voice to do right. When you *do* good, you *feel* good, and that is the Holy Ghost speaking to you. The Holy Ghost is a wonderful companion. He is *always* there to help you.

My dear boys and girls, honor your fathers and mothers. They will help you make good decisions. Enjoy and respect your grandparents. Be a real friend to your brothers and sisters. Choose friends who have high ideals. Choose friends who will help you to be good.

Attend sacrament meeting. Listen carefully to what your bishop says. He is an important spiritual leader who has a special calling from Heavenly Father to help you.

Enjoy Primary, and attend every week. Bring your member and nonmember friends to Primary. Learn the Primary songs well. They are wonderful. Memorize the Articles of Faith and earn the Gospel in Action Award.

Be honest. Do not lie nor steal. Do not cheat. Do not use profanity, but be clean in your thoughts and speech.

Be a *true* Latter-day Saint. Stand up for your beliefs. One of my favorite Primary songs is "Dare to Do Right." Some of the words are,

> Dare to do right! dare to be true!
> You have a work that no other can do;
> Do it so bravely, so kindly, so well,
> Angels will hasten the story to tell.
> (*Sing with Me: Songs for Children* [Salt Lake City: The Church of Jesus Christ of Latter-day Saints, 1969], B-81.)

Remember, Satan does not want you to be happy. He does not want you to dare to do right. He wants you to be miserable, as he is. He has captured the hearts of wicked men and women who would have you participate in bad things such as pornography, drugs, profanity, and immorality. Stay away from these evils. Avoid books, magazines, videos, movies, and television shows that are not good. As the scriptures tell us, avoid the very *appearance* of evil. (See 1 Thes. 5:22.)

Dress modestly. Choose clothing that covers your body properly. Behave in a courteous and polite way. Live the Word of Wisdom. Keep the Sabbath day holy. Listen to good music. Do your best to be good.

Do well in your school work and strive to be a good student.

With help from your parents, begin your own library of favorite tapes, books, and pictures which are available at Church distribution centers. Enjoy reading each month in your home the *Friend* magazine or the international magazines.

Love the country in which you live. Be a good citizen. Be patriotic. Fly your country's flag on special holidays. Pray for your country's leaders.

Primary boys, plan and look forward to serving a full-time mission for the Lord. Young girls, be prepared for missionary service if you are called. But also, young girls, learn from your mothers the important homemaking skills you will use in your own home.

Now I want to say something to you children who do not feel safe and who are frightened or hurt and do not know what to do. Sometimes you may feel all alone. You need to know that even when it seems that no one else cares, your Heavenly Father does. He will always love you. He wants you to be protected and safe. If you are not, please talk to someone who can help you—a parent, a teacher, your bishop, or a friend. They will help you.

I am sure each of you has favorite stories from the scriptures. One of my favorite stories is found in the seventeenth chapter of 3 Nephi in the Book of Mormon. It tells about the visit of Jesus to the people on the American continent after His resurrection. It tells about Jesus healing the sick and teaching the people and praying to Heavenly Father for them.

Now, this is one of my favorite parts of that story:

"And it came to pass that when Jesus had made an end of praying unto the Father, he arose; but so great was the joy of the multitude that they were overcome.

"And it came to pass that Jesus spake unto them, and bade them arise.

"And they arose from the earth, and he said unto them: Blessed are ye because of your faith. And now behold, my joy is full.

"And when he had said these words, he wept, and the multitude bare record of it, and he took their little children, one by one, and blessed them, and prayed unto the Father for them.

"And when he had done this he wept again;

"And he spake unto the multitude, and said unto them: Behold your little ones.

"And as they looked to behold they cast their eyes

towards heaven, and they saw the heavens open, and they saw angels descending out of heaven as it were in the midst of fire; and they came down and encircled those little ones about, and they were encircled about with fire; and the angels did minister unto them." (Vs. 18–24.)

I promise you, dear children, that angels will minister unto you also. You may not see them, but they will be there to help you, and you will feel of their presence.

> Favored little ones were they,
> Who towards him Jesus drew!
> Who within his arms he took
> Just as loving parents do,
> Christ the Lord "Our living head."
> This of little children said.
> "Such shall of my kingdom be,
> Suffer them to come to me."
> Listen to the Savior's plea,
> "Let the children come to me."
> ("Let the Little Children Come," in *Sing with Me*, B-14.)

Dear children, our Heavenly Father sent you to earth at this time because you are some of His most valiant children. He knew there would be much wickedness in the world today, and He knew you could be faithful and obedient.

Dear child, you are God's gift to your parents, and the gift your parents can give God is to bring you back to Him sweet and pure and faithful.

He expects your parents and leaders to teach you, to walk beside you, and to be shining examples to you so that you will know the way you should go. They must spend time with you and love you and pray *with* you and *for* you.

Your leaders must call faithful men and women to teach you in Primary. We must provide experiences for you early in your life that will help you know how to live the gospel.

God bless the children of this Church. How I love you! How Heavenly Father loves you! And may we, as your parents, teachers, and leaders, be *more* child-like — more submissive, more meek, and more humble.

I close my message to you this day with the prayer that we may ever respond to your plea as *you* so sweetly sing:

> Teach me to walk in the light of his love;
> Teach me to pray to my Father above;
> Teach me to know of the things that are right;
> Teach me, teach me to walk in the light.

And then, as your parents, *we* sing to you:

> Come, little child, and together we'll learn
> Of his commandments, that we may return
> Home to his presence, to live in his sight—
> Always, always to walk in the light.

And *together* we sing:

> Father in Heaven, we thank thee this day
> For loving guidance to show us the way.
> Grateful, we praise thee with songs of delight!
> Gladly, gladly we'll walk in the light.
> ("Teach Me to Walk in the Light," in
> *Hymns,* no. 304.)

For this I fervently pray for the children of the Church, in the name of Jesus Christ, amen.

To the Elderly
in the Church

*An address given at the Saturday morning
session of general conference, 30 September 1989*

My beloved brethren and sisters, it is a joy to be able to meet with you again in another glorious general conference of the Church—to feel of your spirit and support and to know of your love of the Lord.

I look forward to hearing the inspiring messages of the General Authorities of the Church. I am so grateful for their sustaining power and in particular for the great help of my noble Counselors and the Quorum of the Twelve.

May I express to them and to all of you my deep appreciation for your kind remembrances to me on my recent ninetieth birthday.

In the past I have directed my remarks to the children of the Church, to the young men and young women, to the single adult brethren and sisters, and to the mothers and fathers in Israel. This morning I would like to speak to the elderly in the Church and to their families and to those who minister to their needs.

I hold special feelings for the elderly—for this marvelous group of men and women. I feel that in some measure I understand them, for I am one of them.

The Lord knows and loves the elderly among His people. It has always been so, and upon them He has bestowed many of His greatest responsibilities. In various dispensations He has guided His people through

71

prophets who were in their advancing years. He has needed the wisdom and experience of age, the inspired direction from those with long years of proven faithfulness to His gospel.

The Lord blessed Sarah, in her old age, to bear Abraham a child. Perhaps King Benjamin's greatest sermon was given when he was very elderly and nigh unto death. He was truly an instrument in the hands of the Lord as he was able to lead and establish peace among his people.

Many other men and women throughout the ages have accomplished great things as they went forth to serve the Lord and His children, even in their elderly years.

In our dispensation, of the thirteen prophets who have been called of the Lord, many were called when they were in their seventies or eighties, or even older. How the Lord knows and loves His children who have given so much through their years of experience!

We love you who are the elderly in the Church. You are the fastest-growing segment of our population in the world today, as well as within the Church.

Our desires are that your golden years will be wonderful and rewarding. We pray that you will feel the joy of a life well-spent and one filled with fond memories and even greater expectations through Christ's atonement. We hope you will feel of the peace the Lord promised those who continue to strive to keep His commandments and follow His example. We hope your days are filled with things to do and ways in which you can render service to others who are not as fortunate as you. Older almost always means better, for your wealth of wisdom and experience can continue to expand and increase as you reach out to others.

May we suggest eight areas in which we can make the most of our senior years:

1. *Work in the temple and attend often.* We who are older should use our energies not only to bless our predecessors, but to ensure that, insofar as possible, all of our posterity might receive the ordinances of exaltation in the temple. Work with your families, counsel with and pray for those who may yet be unwilling to prepare themselves.

We urge all who can to attend the temple frequently and accept calls to serve in the temple when health and strength and distance will permit. We rely on you to help in temple service. With the increasing number of temples, we need more of our members to prepare themselves for this sweet service. Sister Benson and I are grateful that almost every week we can attend the temple together. What a blessing this has been in our lives!

2. *Collect and write family histories.* We call upon you to pursue vigorously the gathering and writing of personal and family histories. In so many instances, you alone have within you the history, the memory of loved ones, the dates and events. In some situations you *are* the family history. In few ways will your heritage be better preserved than by your collecting and writing your histories.

3. *Become involved in missionary service.* We need increasing numbers of senior missionaries in missionary service. Where health and means make it possible, we call upon hundreds more of our couples to set their lives and affairs in order and to go on missions. How we need you in the mission field! You are able to perform missionary service in ways that our younger missionaries cannot.

I'm grateful that two of my own widowed sisters were able to serve as missionary companions together

73

in England. They were sixty-eight and seventy-three years of age when they were called, and they both had a marvelous experience.

What an example and a blessing it is to a family's posterity when grandparents serve missions. Most senior couples who go are strengthened and revitalized by missionary service. Through this holy avenue of service, many are sanctified and feel the joy of bringing others to the knowledge of the fulness of the gospel of Jesus Christ.

Also, through the Family-to-Family Book of Mormon Program, send copies of the Book of Mormon on missions for you with your testimonies enclosed.

4. *Provide leadership by building family togetherness.* We urge all senior members, when possible, to call their families together. Organize them into cohesive units. Give leadership to family gatherings. Establish family reunions where fellowship and family heritage can be felt and learned. Some of the sweetest memories I have are of our own family reunions and gatherings. Foster wonderful family traditions which will bind you together eternally. In doing so, we can create a bit of heaven right here on earth within individual families. After all, eternity will be but an extension of righteous family life.

5. *Accept and fulfill Church callings.* We trust that all senior members who possibly can will accept callings in the Church and fulfill them with dignity. I am grateful to personally know brethren who are in their seventies and eighties who are serving as bishops and branch presidents. How we need the counsel and influence of you who have walked the pathway of life! We all need to hear of your successes and how you have risen above heartache, pain, or disappointment, having become stronger for experiencing them.

There are rich opportunities for you to serve in

74

most of the organizations of the Church. You have the time and solid gospel foundation which enable you to render a great work. In so many ways, you lead out in faithful service in the Church. We thank you for all that you have done and pray that the Lord will strengthen you to do more.

6. *Plan for your financial future.* As you move through life toward retirement and the decades which follow, we invite all of our senior members to plan frugally for the years following full-time employment. Let us avoid unnecessary debt. We also advise caution in cosigning financial notes, even with family members, when retirement income might be jeopardized.

Be even more cautious in advancing years about "get-rich" schemes, mortgaging homes, or investing in uncertain ventures. Proceed cautiously so that the planning of a lifetime is not disrupted by one or a series of poor financial decisions. Plan your financial future early; then follow the plan.

7. *Render Christlike service.* Christlike service exalts. Knowing this, we call upon all senior members who are able to thrust in their sickles in service to others. This can be part of the sanctifying process. The Lord has promised that those who lose their lives serving others will find themselves. The Prophet Joseph Smith told us that we should "wear out our lives" in bringing to pass His purposes. (D&C 123:13.)

Peace and joy and blessings will follow those who render service to others. Yes, we commend Christlike service to all, but it is especially sweet in the lives of the elderly.

8. *Stay physically fit, healthy, and active.* We are thrilled with the efforts being made by so many of the elderly to ensure good health in advancing years. We see many walking in the early mornings. We hear of others who use exercise equipment in their own

75

homes. Some even enter marathons and do remarkably well. Still others have swimming programs to keep them fit. Until recently our own beloved General Authority emeritus, Joseph Anderson, now in his one hundredth year, would swim a mile every day. I am not quite up to that, but I do enjoy a vigorous walk each day, which refreshes me.

How we love to see our elderly remain vigorous and active! Through keeping active, both the mind and the body function better. One stake president reported that one of his members went waterskiing on his eightieth birthday.

To those who have lost your spouses, we should also like to express our love. Sometimes there is for some of you a feeling of uselessness and aloneness which can be almost overwhelming. In so many instances, this need not be so. In addition to the eight major suggestions just mentioned, here is a sampling of activities that have proved helpful to others.

Some who are alone keep busy by quilting blankets for each new grandchild to be married or each new baby born into the family. Others write letters on birthdays or attend school and athletic events of grandchildren when they can. Some compile albums of pictures of each grandchild to give on birthdays. We know of one widowed great-grandmother who teaches piano to nearly thirty students. She has spoken to nearly five thousand youth in the last three years. One of them asked her, "Did you cross the plains with the pioneers?"

We see numerous others of our widows who volunteer as "pink ladies" at the hospitals or render other kinds of community service. So many find fulfillment helping in these ways.

The key to overcoming aloneness and a feeling of uselessness for one who is physically able is to step outside yourself by helping others who are truly needy. We promise those who will render this kind of service that, in some measure, you will be healed of the loss of loved ones or the dread of being alone. The way to feel better about your own situation is to improve someone else's circumstances.

To those who are ill and suffering pain and the vicissitudes of this life, we extend particular love and concern. Our hearts and prayers go out to you. Remember what father Lehi said in blessing his son Jacob, who had suffered at the hands of his older brothers Laman and Lemuel. He said, "Thou knowest the greatness of God; and he shall consecrate thine afflictions for thy gain." (2 Ne. 2:2.) And so he will for you.

We pray that you will continue to strive to remain strong in attitude and spirit. We know it is not always easy. We pray that those who now do for you tasks that you no longer are able to do for yourselves will do so in love, in gentleness, and with a caring spirit.

We hope that you will continue to generate good thoughts and feelings in your heart and mind and quickly dismiss those which are harmful and destructive to you. We trust your prayers are being offered daily and even hourly, if needed. As the Book of Mormon teaches, "Live in thanksgiving daily, for the many mercies and blessings which [God] doth bestow upon you." (Alma 34:38.)

You will find that the daily reading of the Book of Mormon will lift your spirit, draw you nearer to your Savior, and help you to be a student of the gospel who can share great truths with others.

Now for a few minutes may I speak to the families of the elderly. We repeat a scripture from Psalms: "Cast me not off in the time of old age; forsake me not when my strength faileth." (71:9.)

We encourage families to give their elderly parents and grandparents the love, care, and attention they deserve. Let us remember the scriptural command that we must care for those of our own house lest we be found "worse than an infidel." (1 Tim. 5:8.) I am so grateful for my own dear family and for the loving care they have given their parents over so many years.

Remember, parents and grandparents are our responsibility, and we are to care for them to the very best of our ability. When the elderly have no families to care for them, priesthood and Relief Society leaders should make every effort to meet their needs in the same loving way. We submit a few suggestions to families of the elderly.

Ever since the Lord etched the Ten Commandments into the tablets of stone, His words from Sinai have echoed down through the centuries to "Honour thy father and thy mother." (Ex. 20:12.)

To honor and respect our parents means that we have a high regard for them. We love and appreciate them and are concerned about their happiness and well-being. We treat them with courtesy and thoughtful consideration. We seek to understand their points of view. Certainly obedience to parents' righteous desires and wishes is a part of honoring.

Furthermore, our parents deserve our honor and respect for giving us life itself. Beyond this, they have almost always made countless sacrifices as they cared for and nurtured us through our infancy and childhood, provided us with the necessities of life, and nursed us through physical illnesses and the emotional stresses of growing up. In many instances, they provided us with the opportunity to receive an education, and, in a measure, they educated us. Much of what we know and do we learned from their example. May we ever be grateful to them and show that gratitude.

Let us also learn to be forgiving of our parents, who, perhaps having made mistakes as they reared us, almost always did the best they knew how. May we ever forgive them as we would likewise wish to be forgiven by our own children for mistakes we make.

Even when parents become elderly, we ought to honor them by allowing them freedom of choice and the opportunity for independence as long as possible. Let us not take away from them choices that they can still make. Some parents are able to live and care for themselves well into their advancing years and would prefer to do so. Where they can, let them.

If they become less able to live independently, then family, Church, and community resources may be needed to help them. When the elderly become unable to care for themselves, even with supplemental aid, care can be provided in the home of a family member when possible. Church and community resources may also be needed in this situation.

The role of the care-giver is vital. There is great need for support and help to be given to such a person. Usually this is an elderly spouse or a middle-aged daughter with children of her own to care for as well as caring for the elderly parent.

We also hope that you would include the elderly in family activities when possible. What a joy it is for us to see lively, sweet grandchildren with a loving grandparent in the midst of them. Children love such occasions. They love to have their grandparents visit them and to have them over for dinner, for family home evenings, and on other special events. This provides opportunities for teaching ways to honor, love, respect, and care for those who are in their later years.

Grandparents can have a profound influence on their grandchildren. Their time is generally not as encumbered and busy as the parents', so books can be opened and read, stories can be told, and application of gospel principles taught. Children then obtain a perspective of life which is not only rewarding but can also bring them security, peace, and strength. It is possible to send letters, tapes, and pictures, particularly where distances are great and it is not possible to see one another often. Those who are blessed with a closeness to grandparents and other elderly people have a rich companionship and association. There might be times when they can attend graduations, weddings, temple excursions, missionary farewells and homecomings, and other special events with family members.

We enjoy watching our children and grandchildren grow and achieve in special ways, as we share in many of their joys and rejoice in their victories. Happiness blesses our lives as our children strive and achieve in their own lives. In 3 John 1:4 we read, "I have no greater joy than to hear that my children walk in truth." And knowing this can bring a renewal of love and courage to continue in our own struggles.

Finally, we would urge priesthood leaders of the elderly to be sensitive to the Spirit of our Father in Heaven in assessing and meeting the spiritual, physical, emotional, and financial needs of the elderly. We trust you will utilize your counselors, Melchizedek Priesthood quorum leaders, and Relief Society leaders, home teachers, and visiting teachers in this great responsibility, for we must fulfill these duties without reluctance or hesitation.

We hope that priesthood and auxiliary leaders will

continue to give the elderly callings in which they can use their reservoirs of wisdom and counsel. We hope, where possible, that each can be a home teacher or visiting teacher. Even those who are somewhat confined to their beds and homes can sometimes assist in this watchcare through telephone calls, writing notes, or other special assignments.

A priesthood leader can do much to assist and encourage individuals and couples as they prepare to serve missions. The temple extraction and welfare programs are blessed greatly by those who are in their senior years and have opportunities to serve in this area.

We hope each of the elderly individuals and couples has sensitive and caring home teachers and visiting teachers assigned to them. Great comfort and peace can come to those who know they have someone to whom they can turn in time of emergency or need. It is important that tact, diplomacy, and sincerity be evident in assessing and addressing such needs.

We hope you will involve the independent elderly in compassionate service assignments. Include them also in stake and ward social activities, especially single members and those with dependent spouses. So many times they are forgotten. Especially at the time of the death of a spouse, loving care can be given. This is a very tender time for most.

At times temporary relief is very much needed and appreciated by family members who provide constant physical and emotional care to those with special needs. It is important to help the family maintain its functions as a family with periodic freedom from the heavy responsibilities that long-term or terminal illness can impose. All need loving support and relief from the overwhelming duties of serious illness or problems.

Transportation is often a great concern to the elderly. We can assist by providing a way for them to attend their Sunday meetings, visit loved ones, shop, and go to the doctor or clinic.

Again, we should prayerfully seek inspiration and direction in caring for the elderly. There is always a great diversity of individuals and individual needs.

God bless the elderly in the Church. I love you with all my heart. I am one of you.

You have so much to live for. May these golden years be your very best years as you fully live and love and serve. And God bless those who minister to your needs—your family, your friends, and your fellow Church members and leaders.

I leave you my testimony of the joy of living—of the joys of *full* gospel living and of going through the Refiner's fire and the sanctification process that takes place. As the Apostle Paul so well said, "We know that all things work together for good to them that love God." (Rom. 8:28.)

I leave my blessing upon you. The Savior lives. This is His church. The work is true, and in the words of our Lord and Savior, "Look unto me, and endure to the end, and ye shall live; for unto him that endureth to the end will I give eternal life" (3 Ne. 15:9), to which I testify in the name of Jesus Christ, amen.

Index

before mission call, 18; for
marriage, 50, 57; qualities
to look for in partner
while, 54, 57–58
Discipline, 45

Elderly: contributions of,
71–72, 78–79; eight
suggestions for, 73–76; to
do family history work, 73;
missionary work of, 73–74;
service of, 74–77, 81;
overcoming loneliness of,
76–77; who suffer, 77; care
of, by their families, 77–80;
honoring of, 78–79; who
are grandparents, 79–80;
priesthood leaders to
assist, 80–82; blessing on,
82
Enduring to end, 82
Entertainment, 7–8, 20–21, 66

Faith to marry, 53
Family: strengthening of, 2,
14–15; activities of, 33–34,
74; preparedness of, 42;
children to honor, 65;
histories of, 73; elderly to
organize, 74; to care for
elderly, 77–80. *See also*
Children; Fathers; Mothers
Fathers: responsibility of, for
sons, 9–10; role and calling
of, 26, 37, 39–40, 45–47; to
invite children into family,
26–28; to provide
financially, 29–30, 40–42;
to provide spiritual
leadership, 42–43, 45–47;
to love spouses, 43–44;
ways for, to lead children,
45–46
Finances, planning, 75
First Presidency, 3–4, 16
Fitness, physical, 75–76

Food storage, 42
Forgiveness, 79
Freedom of elderly, 79
Friends, being, to children, 32
Future, financial, 75

Goals, suggested, 46, 51,
73–76
Gospel, teaching, 34–35
Grandparents, 79–80

Health, 75–76
Helaman, sons of, 1–2
Holy Ghost, 65
Home, mothers to stay in,
29–32, 40–42
Home teachers, 80–81
Honoring of parents, 78–79
Husbands: to provide for
family, 28–31, 40–42; to
love wives, 43–44. *See also*
Fathers

Immorality, 5–7, 18–21
Independence of elderly, 79

Jesus Christ, 43, 67–68, 59

Kimball, Spencer W.: read
scriptures as boy, 2–3, 15;
on not committing sin, 6,
19; on sexual sin, 7, 19–20;
on dating, 8, 21–22; on
mothers at home, 30–31;
on starting families, 41; on
delaying marriage, 52–53

Leaders, Church: to help
youth, 1, 9–10, 23–24; to
help children, 68–69; who
are elderly, 71–72; to help
the elderly, 80–82
Leadership, fathers to provide
spiritual, 42–43, 45–47;
through love, 43–44
Lee, Harold B., 39